Vi̶c̶t̶o̶r̶i̶a̶n̶ Life

Transport

Nicola Barber

WAYLAND

First published in 2008
by Wayland

Copyright © Wayland 2008

Editor: Katie Powell
Designer: Jane Hawkins
Concept design: Paul Cherrill

Wayland
338 Euston Road
London NW1 3BH

Wayland Australia
Level 17/207 Kent Street
Sydney, NSW 2000

British Library Cataloguing in Publication Data

Barber, Nicola
  Transport. - (Victorian life)
  1. Transportation - Great Britain - History - 19th century
  - Juvenile literature 2. Great Britain - Social life and
  customs - 19th century - Juvenile literature
  I. Title
  388'.0941'09034

ISBN 978 0 7502 5366 6

Picture acknowledgements: Bridgeman Art Library/English
School/Getty Images: 14, City of London/HIP/TopFoto.co.uk:
6, 19, Mary Evans ILN Pictures: 11, 22, 23, Mary Evans Picture
Library: 8, 9, 12, 17, Hulton Archive/Getty Images: COVER
(main image), 16, 26, Institution of Civil Engineers/Mary Evans
Picture Library: 18, 21, 28T, Lebrecht Music and Arts Photo
Library/Alamy: 3, 15, Lordprice Collection/Alamy: 20, Bill
Meadows/Mary Evans Picture Library: 13,Motoring Picture Library:
27, National Archives/HIP/TopFoto.co.uk: COVER (BR), 4, 25, 28B,
Topham Picturepoint/TopFoto.co.uk: 24, Wayland Archive: 5, 7, 10

Printed in China

Wayland is a division of Hachette Children's Books,
an Hachette Livre UK company
www.hachettelivre.co.uk

Contents

Words in **bold** can be found
in the glossary.

Changing Britain

The long **reign** of Queen Victoria was a time of great change in Britain and the development of transport played a major part in these changes.

Britain becomes a world power

Industrial and economic advances that helped to make Britain a world power in the nineteenth century were made possible by the improvement of roads, the construction of a railway network and breakthroughs in forms of transport.

Changing Britain

When Queen Victoria came to the throne in 1837, most people lived in the countryside and rarely travelled further than their nearest town. By the time of her death in 1901, Britain's population had more than doubled. Roughly three-quarters of these people lived and worked in the country's cities. The construction of the railways made short-distance commuting and long-distance travel possible for people from all social classes.

Queen Victoria sits in the royal carriage with her husband Prince Albert and King Louis-Philippe of France.

The Industrial Revolution

The development of transport went hand-in-hand with the **Industrial Revolution**. This so-called 'revolution' started in the late eighteenth century with the invention of machines that could perform jobs previously done by hand, and was already well under way when Victoria came to the throne.

Engineers such as Richard Trevithick (1771–1833) developed steam engines to power machinery in the new mills and factories. Soon steam was being used to drive moving engines too (see page 12). The need to move heavy loads from one part of the country to another had led to the construction of a canal network in the late eighteenth century, and the first **locomotives** were also developed to transport heavy loads such as coal and stone.

George Stephenson, 1781–1848

George Stephenson was known to the Victorians as the 'father of railways'. His father worked at a coal mine, and from a very early age George was fascinated by machines. George started work at the mine too when he was 14, and taught himself about machines by taking them to pieces and putting them back together again. He went on to develop the first steam-powered locomotive to run on tracks, and worked on the first public railways with his son, Robert (see page 13).

⬆ The Great Exhibition celebrated Britain's status as a centre of industrial development. It was held in Crystal Palace, Hyde Park, London, in 1851.

Horse power

Before the railways were built in Britain, the horse was a vital means of transport. Horses were used in towns and rural areas to transport goods and people. Many wealthy people kept horses and carriages for their own use.

Fast and slow

For long-distance travel, teams of strong, fast horses pulled **stage coaches**. Stage coaches carried paying passengers, parcels and post from town to town. **Carrier's wagons** were much slower and were only used for local journeys. Horses and carts were also used to transport goods in rural areas and for work on farms.

⬇ A carrier's wagon makes slow progress along a lane compared to the train in the background.

A day in the life of...

...a stage coach driver:

'My name is Sam Haywood and I drive the stage coach known to all as 'the Wonder'. My route lies between the 'Hen and Chickens' in Birmingham and the 'Lion' in Shrewsbury. The arrival of the stage coach in Shrewsbury every night is a spectacle and I'm proud of it. We cross the English Bridge and then gallop at a fine pace up Wyle Cop, finishing at a trot as we pass through the archway of the Lion Hotel. My passengers must take care not to stick out their heads lest they receive a knock – the archway is just inches wider than my coach.'

Travelling by stage coach

When Queen Victoria came to the British throne in 1837, a network of stage coaches was well established. They were driven by coachmen and often protected from highwaymen by guards who carried pistols. Coaching inns across the network had stable yards so that tired horses could be changed for fresh ones and food, drink, and often a bed, could be offered to passengers. Seats could be reserved on stage coaches at the coaching inns, and smaller carriages could be hired to take people to their final destinations. With the arrival of the railways, stage coaches were no longer needed, as travel by train was quicker, cheaper and far more comfortable.

⇧ A stage coach draws up outside a coaching inn on the outskirts of London in 1900.

Victorian canals

The great age of canal building began just before the Victorian era, in the late eighteenth century. Rivers and canals provided vital transport links during the Industrial Revolution.

Trent and Mersey Canal

In Staffordshire, for example, the potter Josiah Wedgwood supported the building of the Trent and Mersey Canal, which opened in 1777, as it meant he could transport his delicate china goods safely to and from his factory.

Victorian canals

During the Victorian era, the railways were in competition with the canals. Canal boats, called **barges**, were pulled by horses, and therefore moved at a slow walking pace. However from 1880, some boats started to be powered by steam.

⬇ Horses were used to pull heavily laden barges along the canals.

Although the railways could carry bigger loads more quickly, canals in industrial areas continued to be used throughout the nineteenth century to carry goods to and from mills and factories. Loads such as coal, clay, wool and iron were all transported by water. Some new canals were also constructed. The Manchester Ship Canal was opened in 1894. It allowed large ships to go directly to the docks in Manchester, bypassing the nearby city port of Liverpool.

Canal features

The landscape often provided a challenge for canal builders. When planning the most direct route across hilly countryside, the canal builders used **locks** to raise and lower barges from one level to another. In some places, the difference in level was so large that canals were built with several locks, known as a flight of locks. Other features used to overcome the landscape included long tunnels and **aqueducts**, such as the 35 metre (116 foot) high Pontcysyllte Aqueduct which opened in 1805, on the Llangollen Canal in Wales.

Navvies start work on the construction of the Manchester Ship Canal in 1887. Digging out the channels for new canals was back-breaking work.

Building the railways

During the eighteenth century, steam was increasingly used to power engines. It was also used to drive small locomotives that transported heavy loads in quarries and mines. By the early nineteenth century these engines were put to work to power machinery in mills and factories.

GEORGE STEPHENSON.

FIRST LOCOMOTIVE ENGINE.

Improvements to the steam locomotive

Meanwhile, engineers such as George Stephenson and Richard Trevithick were constantly working on improvements to the steam locomotive and, in 1825, the first public railway opened between Stockton and Darlington. On its first journey along the 40 kilometre (26 mile) line, the locomotive, called *Locomotion*, achieved a top speed of 24 kilometres per hour (15 miles per hour).

Speedy machines

Four years later, George and Robert Stephenson's locomotive *The Rocket* set a record of 47 kilometres per hour (29 miles per hour), at speed trials held in Rainhill near Liverpool.

An image of George Stephenson together with his famous *Rocket* locomotive.

Robert Stephenson, 1803–1859

Both Robert Stephenson and his father George were key figures in the development of the railways. Robert worked in partnership with his father on projects such as the Stockton and Darlington Railway. In 1823, the Stephensons founded the first company to build railway locomotives, based in Newcastle-upon-Tyne. Robert was appointed chief engineer on the London to Birmingham line which was completed in 1838. He also built some spectacular railway bridges, including the Britannia Bridge in 1850, across the Menai Strait between the island of Anglesey and mainland Wales.

Passenger trains

In 1830, passenger lines opened between Canterbury and Whitstable in Kent, and between Liverpool and Manchester. Long-distance lines between London and several cities were also opened during the Victorian era. Isambard Kingdom Brunel was chief engineer on the Great Western Railway, which connected London to Bristol in 1841, and later to Exeter in 1844. The line was widely admired for its technical achievements, particularly the Box Tunnel near Bath. At 2,937 metres (9,636 feet), it was the longest railway tunnel in the world at the time.

Isambard Kingdom Brunel's famous Box Tunnel took five years to build. Work began in 1836 and finished in 1841.

Rail travel

Between 1825 and the 1840s, the speed of railway building in Britain was breathtaking. By 1845 there was about 3,927 kilometres (2,440 miles) of railway, carrying 30 million passengers each year.

A royal journey

Queen Victoria made her first rail journey in 1842. She travelled from Slough to Paddington in a carriage especially designed for her by Isambard Kingdom Brunel. The royal party was accompanied by Brunel himself, who wanted to ensure that nothing went wrong. The queen was "quite charmed" by the experience, and used the railways frequently for the rest of her reign, particularly for travel between London and Balmoral Castle, her home in Scotland.

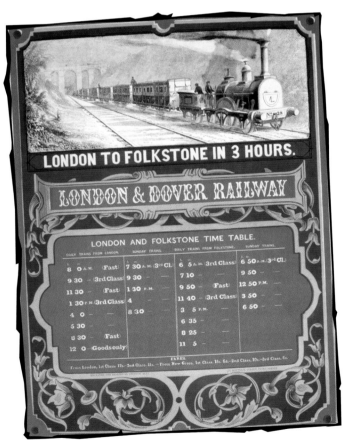

LONDON TO FOLKSTONE IN 3 HOURS.

LONDON & DOVER RAILWAY

LONDON AND FOLKSTONE TIME TABLE.

⬆ An early timetable for the London to Dover line. Cheap train travel meant that many people could visit the seaside for the first time.

Safety and accidents

In 1844, parliament passed the Railway Act that required all railway companies to run at least one passenger train every day, at the cheap rate of one penny per mile. The Act also ensured some basic standards of comfort and safety. However, there were frequent accidents on the railways, often a result of poor brakes or collisions because of a lack of signalling.

Written at the time

One of the worst accidents occurred in 1874 near Norwich, killing and injuring many passengers. The disaster was reported in the *Illustrated London News* on 19 September:

'A mistaken order from Mr. T. Cooper, the night inspector at Norwich station, allowed the down express to leave Norwich, while the combined mail-train from Great Yarmouth was suffered to come on from Brundall. The consequence was that the doomed trains met at Thorpe ... and ran headlong into each other. The rails were slippery from rain; there was a slight curve in the line at the fatal spot, so that the lights of neither train could be seen; there was no time to apply the brakes, and the two engines rushed at each other at full speed.'

Days out

Despite these hazards, rail travel was immensely popular. For the first time, it became possible for everyone to travel long distances. The railway took people on holidays to the seaside, and in 1851, **excursion** trains carried many of the 6 million visitors who attended the Great Exhibition at Crystal Palace in London. Comfort for passengers improved as the Victorian era progressed. But it was not until the 1860s, that the first toilets were installed on trains, and in 1873 sleeping cars were introduced on the London to Glasgow line.

⬆ Early third-class carriages did not have roofs, so passengers were exposed to the wind and rain as they travelled.

Getting about town

For many people living in the crowded and filthy streets of Victorian Britain, the only way to get around was by foot. For those who could afford it however, there were horse-drawn buses and later **tramways**.

People hired hansom cabs to transport them around the city streets. This photograph was taken in 1877 on a London street.

Horse-buses

The first horse-drawn buses in London appeared in 1829, and by the beginning of Victoria's reign there were bus services in most large towns and cities. There were no bus stops – if a passenger wanted to ride on a bus he or she stepped out into the road and 'hailed' it by raising a hand. A conductor travelled at the back of the bus to collect fares, which were typically quite expensive – about 5 pence to travel 5 kilometres (3 miles).

Tramways

In the 1860s, tramways began to appear in Britain's towns and cities. Tramways were first built in the United States in the 1830s, and brought to Britain by an American **entrepreneur** called George Train.

Written at the time

In an essay, the architect H.B. Cresswell describes the dirt and smell of Victorian London in the 1890s:

'But the mud! And the noise! And the smell! All these blemishes were [the] mark of [the] horse ... The whole of London's crowded wheeled traffic—which in parts of the City was at times dense beyond movement—was dependent on the horse: lorry, wagon, bus ... coaches and carriages and private vehicles of all kinds, were appendages [attachments] to horses.'

The trams were pulled by horses along rails in the road. The rails made the trams easier to pull as the tram wheels glided smoothly along, rather than bumping across holes in the roads. Trams quickly became popular because they were cheaper than horse-buses. The first tram to be driven by electricity opened in 1885, in Blackpool. Its power came from a system beneath the rails, but it was the overhead cables, which first supplied power to electric trams in Leeds in 1891, which became widespread.

⬆ London followed Leeds' example and had overhead electric trams by the end of the Victorian era.

The Underground

Road traffic in Britain's towns and cities became a major problem during the Victorian era. In London, the overcrowded streets became such a hazard that in 1860, work began on an underground transport system for the city.

The Metropolitan Railway

The world's first underground railway, called the Metropolitan Railway, opened in London in 1863. The track was laid in shallow trenches which were then roofed over – a method of construction called 'cut and cover'.

The trains were powered by steam, which filled the tunnels and stations of this early underground with a foul-smelling **smog**. Nevertheless, the underground was very popular. Another line was opened five years later, and by 1884, the two were linked to form what is today the Circle Line on London's underground system.

⇧ Workers construct a tunnel for London's new underground system in the 1860s.

The tube

'Cut and cover' construction was disruptive as it often required the demolition of houses or destruction of roads. Engineers began to dig underground to create tunnels instead.

The railways built in these tunnels were called tube railways. In Liverpool, the Mersey Railway Tunnel was dug underneath the River Mersey and opened in 1886. In Glasgow, an underground system was opened in 1896. It used a thick steel rope, called a cable, pulled by a locomotive to haul the trains along. In 1890, the City and South London Railway opened in London. It used electricity to power its trains, and had lifts to carry its passengers between the surface and the stations underground.

A train approaches as passengers wait in Baker Street Station on the Metropolitan Line in 1865.

Written at the time

In his diary, an American journalist called R. D. Blumenfeld describes his experience of travelling on the underground in 1887:

'I got into the Underground railway at Baker Street. I wanted to go to Moorgate Street in the City ... The compartment in which I sat was filled with passengers who were smoking pipes, as is the British habit ... by the time we reached Moorgate Street I was near dead of asphyxiation and heat. I should think these Underground railways must soon be discontinued, for they are a menace to health.'

Steamships

Steamships were first developed in the eighteenth century and by the time Queen Victoria came to the throne, ships driven by steam were in use in many parts of the world.

Paddle steamers

On these steamships, the steam was used to drive large paddle wheels on either side of the ship. The ships carried sails, too, and the first steamship to make a transatlantic crossing in 1819, the *Savannah*, actually used steam for only a small part of the trip.

Transatlantic rivalry

In the 1830s, several companies wanted to be the first to start regular transatlantic steamship services. In 1838, the British and American Steam Navigation Company started its service with the ship *Sirius*. It became the first ship to cross the Atlantic entirely by steam. Its record of 18 days was immediately broken by the larger SS *Great Western*, which made the trip from Bristol to New York in just 15 days.

The SS *Great Britain* at its launch in 1843. Today, this ship is restored and back where it was originally built in Bristol.

Brunel pictured in front of the anchor chains belonging to the SS *Great Eastern*.

While *Sirius* had run out of coal during its crossing, forcing its crew to burn cabin furniture to complete the journey, the SS *Great Western* arrived with coal to spare.

Brunel's ships

The SS *Great Western* was the first of the three magnificent steamships designed by the engineer Isambard Kingdom Brunel. The SS *Great Britain*, launched in Bristol in 1843, was at that time the largest ship in the world. Built of iron, the ship was designed for the luxury transatlantic route, although it also carried passengers to Australia. Brunel's last ship was the SS *Great Eastern*, which was built on the River Thames in London. It was a gigantic ship, made to carry 4,000 passengers and enough coal to sail to Australia without stopping. Although the SS *Great Eastern* never became a passenger ship, its place in history was assured when it was used to lay the first transatlantic **telegraph** cable in 1866.

Isambard Kingdom Brunel, 1806–1859

Brunel was one of the greatest engineers of the nineteenth century. He helped his father, who was also an engineer, with the design and construction of a tunnel under the Thames which opened in 1843. In 1831, Brunel won a competition to design a bridge across the gorge of the River Avon in Bristol. The Clifton Suspension Bridge eventually opened in 1864. Brunel went on to build railways and the three great steamships of the Victorian era. However, work on the SS Great Eastern proved too much for his delicate health, and he died just before its launch in 1859.

The age of sail

While the Victorian age was famous for its huge steamships, it was also known as an age of sail. The transport of goods and people by sea and inland waterways was widespread.

Coastal and inland

Small ships were used for a wide variety of purposes around the coast of Great Britain. Ships such as **wherries** were used to carry goods from port to port, or from larger ships to destinations inland. In many places, **ferries** were used to transport people across rivers. Some ferries could carry horses and carriages as well as people. Ferries were usually rowed or pushed across with poles, although steam-powered ferries came into service later in the Victorian age.

This engraving from the *London Illustrated News* shows emigrants boarding a ship bound for Australia in 1852.

Around the world

The fastest sailing ships were known as 'clippers'. These were large, narrow ships with several masts. They were built to transport people, mail and lucrative cargoes such as wool, tea and spices. The best known were the China clippers, also called the tea clippers, because they transported valuable cargoes of tea from China to Europe. Competition was often fierce between tea clippers belonging to rival companies, and in 1866, 16 tea clippers took part in the Great Tea Race to cover the 24,000 kilometres (15,000 miles) from China to Britain as fast as possible. The winners made the journey in just 90 days.

The *Taeping* and the *Ariel* sail neck and neck up the English Channel at the end of the Great Tea Race in 1866. ⬇

Written at the time

A report in the *Daily Telegraph* of 1866 describes the arrival of the leaders in the Great Tea Race:

'Leaving China at the same time, [the four ships] sailed almost neck-and-neck the whole way, and finally arrived in the London docks within two hours of each other. The 'Taeping', which won, arrived on the Lizard at literally the same hour as the 'Ariel', her nearest rival, and then dashed up the Channel, the two ships abreast of each other. During the entire day they gallantly ran side by side, carried on by a strong westerly wind, every stitch of canvas set, and the sea sweeping their decks as they careered before the gale.'

Bicycles

Bicycles first appeared before Queen Victoria's reign, when a German inventor designed a two-wheeled wooden machine that was pushed along by the rider's legs.

The hobbyhorse

When this early bicycle was introduced in Britain in 1819, it became known as the hobbyhorse. Bicycles became increasingly popular with both men and women as their design improved throughout the Victorian era.

The boneshaker

The next major development, in the 1860s, was a bicycle with pedals. Designed in France, this bicycle was made from metal and was called the velocipede, although in Britain it was nicknamed the boneshaker because its metal wheels gave a very uncomfortable and bone-shaking ride.

This photograph of a penny farthing bicycle dates from the late 1870s.

Riding the ordinary

The success of the boneshaker led to the development of new models. The ordinary, also called the penny farthing, had a huge front wheel which increased the distance covered by one turn of the pedals. It was frightening to ride, however, because it was fast, and the seat was so high above the ground. Most women, hampered by their long skirts, preferred the more stable high tricycles.

A safer model

The development in 1885 of a safer model, called the Rover safety bicycle, was a turning point in the history of the bicycle. The safety bicycle had two wheels the same size and a chain to turn the back wheel. The addition of **pneumatic** tyres in 1888, made the bicycle more comfortable.

The safety bicycle gave a new freedom to both men and women.

Written at the time

This report from the *Liverpool Mercury* describes a bicycle race between Chester and Liverpool held in 1869:

'A considerable gathering of spectators was expected, but scarcely anyone imagined that there would have been such an enormous crowd of persons assembled to see this novel contest. The competitors were announced to start from Chester about half past two o'clock, but long before that time thousands of people, rich and poor, thronged the Chester-road for miles ... Besides pedestrians, there were vehicles of all sorts and sizes—bicycles, carriages, cars, gigs, spring carts, donkey carts, etc.'

The first cars

While steam engines were used to propel trains and ships, steam-powered road vehicles were not so successful. Early attempts in Britain to build steam-powered cars often ended in explosions or accidents.

Traction engines

Steam-driven vehicles were limited to powerful, but slow and heavy **traction engines** which, from the 1870s onwards, were used on farms and for hauling heavy loads.

A breakthrough

In the 1880s, a German engineer called Karl Benz developed the first practical petrol-driven engine. Benz built and drove the earliest motor car in 1885. By 1888, motor cars were being produced in Germany for sale. In 1895, a French rubber manufacturing company called Michelin developed the first tyres for cars filled with **compressed air**.

⬅ This photograph of an early motor car dates from 1895.

Written at the time

The earliest cars were very expensive, and only the wealthy could afford to buy them. In 1900, Queen Victoria's eldest son, the Prince of Wales (later King Edward VII) ordered a Daimler car, built in Coventry. In 1901, his wife Princess Alexandra wrote about it in a letter to him:

'... I did enjoy being driven about in the cool of the evening at 50 miles!! an hour! – when nothing in the way of course only! and I must say I have the greatest confidence in our driver – I poke him violently in the back at every corner to go gently and whenever a dog, child or anything else comes in our way!'

The red flag

In Britain, a law known as the Red Flag Act was passed in 1865. It limited the speed of any horse-less road vehicle to 6.4 kilometres per hour (4 miles per hour) in open country and 3.2 kilometeres per hour (2 miles per hour) in towns, and required that there be two people in the vehicle and one to walk ahead of it carrying a red flag. This act restricted the earliest motor cars in Britain, and when it was changed in 1896, a celebratory rally was held as 33 motor cars drove from London to Brighton.

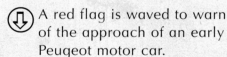 A red flag is waved to warn of the approach of an early Peugeot motor car.

Timeline

1837   Queen Victoria comes to the throne.

1837   The launch of Brunel's SS *Great Western*.

1838   The London to Birmingham Railway opens.

1841   The Great Western Railway opens between London and Bristol. It was extended to Exeter in 1844.

1842   Queen Victoria makes her first journey by train.

1843   The launch of the SS *Great Britain*.

1844   The Railway Act ensures some cheap travel on all railway lines.

1850   Robert Stephenson's Britannia Bridge across the Menai Strait opens.

1851   The Great Exhibition takes place at Crystal Palace in Hyde Park, London.

1859   The launch of the SS *Great Eastern*.

1863   The opening of the first underground railway – the Metropolitan Railway in London.

1864   Brunel's Clifton Suspension Bridge in Bristol opens.

1865   The Red Flag Act limits the speed of horse-less vehicles on Britain's roads.

1866   The Great Tea Race from China to Britain.

1866   The SS *Great Eastern* successfully lays the first transatlantic telegraph cable.

1885   The first trams to be driven by electricity start in Blackpool.

1885   The Rover safety bicycle is invented.

1885   Karl Benz builds the first practical motor car.

1890   The first deep underground railway – the City and South London Railway opens.

1891   The first trams to use the overhead trolley system begin to operate in Leeds.

1896   The repeal of the Red Flag Act.

1901   The death of Queen Victoria.

Glossary

aqueduct a bridge that carries water, either a waterway such as a canal, or a water supply

barge a long flat-bottomed boat

carrier wagon a sturdy wagon pulled by a horse and used to carry heavy loads

clipper a fast sailing ship

compressed air air that is squashed to take up less space

entrepreneur someone who is prepared to take risks in business in order to make a profit

excursion a short journey or outing, such as a day trip

ferry a boat that is used to take people and sometimes vehicles across short stretches of water, such as a river

Industrial Revolution the name given to a time when steam-powered machinery was developed to do jobs previously done by hand. The Industrial Revolution took place in Britain during the end of the eighteenth and the beginning of the nineteenth centuries

lock on a canal, a lock is a place with gates at either end. When both gates are shut the water level is lowered or raised to allow boats to move between canals at two different levels

locomotive a machine that moves trains on a railway track

navvy short for 'navigator', the name given to a man who worked on the construction of the canals, and later the railways and other construction projects

pneumatic something that is filled with compressed air

reign the number of years a king or queen rules over a country

smog a mixture of thick fog and air pollution

stage coach a large carriage pulled by horses that carried passengers, mail and parcels

telegraph messages sent along a wire

traction engine a large, heavy vehicle powered by steam

tramway a public transport system that uses rails set into the roads along which vehicles called trams can run

wherry a small sailing boat used for transporting goods

Index

Resources

History Detective: Victorian Transport Colin Stott, Wayland 2002
Facts About: The Victorians Kay Woodward, Wayland 2007
The Victorians reconstructed Liz Gogerly, Wayland 2005

www.bbc.co.uk/schools/victorians
An excellent website that summarises Victorian life.
www.victorianweb.org
Explore many different topics about the Victorians.